The Immersion Blender Cookbook

By Marian Getz

ACKNOWLEDGEMENTS

A most sincere thank you to our wonderful HSN customers for without you, there would be no cookbook.

Thank you Wolfgang, for your passionate leadership. To be able to work with you makes me the luckiest person I know. There is no other chef in the whole world that I would rather work for. I respect you and am incredibly proud to work for you. Your witty sense of humor is just the icing on the cake.

To my husband Greg, your love is my most cherished recipe of all. Thanks honey for finding the ways to encourage me, for nudging me onward and for telling me I can do it even when I don't believe it myself. You are the best part of me. Thanks also for so sweetly sharing the couch with me and my invasive, teetering stacks of cookbooks.

To my beloved children Jordan and Ben, what a joy it is to experience life with you as adults. You make everything in life better.

To my daughter-in-law Lindsay, I love you and thanks for sharing your creative talent by prop styling for the cookbooks.

To David, Adele and John for teasing me like all siblings should, and for pretending not to mind all the extra dishes I made that we had to wash. I love you all.

To my sister, Janet, who is profoundly mentally retarded. For that reason, I did not have the pleasure of growing up beside you. I can't wait to bake for you in heaven.

To Mom and Dad, one of the greatest influences you have had on my life is through the beautiful example of your love for one another.

When you are lucky enough to work for Wolfgang Puck, you are also ever so fortunate to work with the likes of Sydney Silverman, Mike Sanseverino, Jonathan Schwartz, Arnie Simon, Phoebe Soong, Nicolle Brown and many other wonderful people at the office.

Special thanks to our editor and photographer Daniel Koren. Thank you for your gentle patience and for giving my garbled words and scribbled recipes a sweet voice and a story. You take such beautiful photographs. You have taken my humble food and captured it on film so that each photo makes me hungry.

During the early days of my cooking career, many kitchen tasks were tedious work. I had aching arms from whisking dressings by hand and spent hours chopping garlic or passing ingredients trough a food mill. Life back then would have been so much easier with an immersion blender.

Having an immersion blender in your kitchen is like having a sous chef or a prep cook by your side. Marian really showcases what the immersion blender can do. Her cookbook will not only save you an enormous amount of time, but will also inspire you to become a better cook.

A student of cooking is probably one of the best ways to describe Marian. She is always looking for something new, something fresh, something local and something seasonal. Her culinary knowledge combined with her passion for cooking is second to none and this book will motivate you to be more creative in the kitchen.

Wolfgang Puck

INTRODUCTION

TABLE OF CONTENTS

IMMERSION BLENDER TIPS

Soups

When puréeing hot soup, always start off on the lowest speed to control potential splashing and steam. Increase speed once ingredients are puréed.

Use Caution

Use caution when dealing with hot baked goods as they can produce burns if not handled correctly. Keep a pair of hand mitts or pot holders nearby.

Even Baking

To ensure even baking, rotate the baking sheets from the top rack to the bottom rack and turn the trays around halfway in the middle of the baking cycle.

Overmixing

Watch closely when using your immersion blender. It operates so fast that it can be easy to overmix some recipes like whipped cream. Always monitor the mixing closely.

Testing for Doneness

To test cakes for doneness, insert a toothpick or bamboo skewer off center. When pulling it back out, it should generally come out with just a few moist crumbs clinging to it. For custards, insert a knife off center and it should come out clean. For breads, bake until the internal temperature registers 200 degrees on a thermometer. For frying in oil, always use caution and a deep frying thermometer to monitor the oil temperature. For cookies, pizzas and pastries, look for slight puffing and brown color.

Stickiness

Use parchment paper, non-stick spray or the new aluminum foil that is coated with silicone. It makes sticking a thing of the past and will make baking things like cookies or pastries so much easier.

Chocolate

Buy good quality chocolate and cocoa. It is easy to find excellent chocolate at most grocery stores. Good quality cocoa is harder to find so I order mine online. See the source page 140.

Vanilla

Tahitian vanilla beans and extracts are among the best in the world. You can find a supplier on the source page 140. Use them in recipes where the vanilla flavor takes center stage. If vanilla is not the star flavor, like in the Chocolate Crinkle Cookies on page 85, use imitation vanilla. It adds the correct taste and aroma and is far less expensive. I also love a great inexpensive imitation flavoring called Magic Line Butter Vanilla Extract.

Butter

All of the butter used in this book is unsalted. Softened butter means butter that has been left at room temperature for several hours. It should be soft enough to offer no resistance when sliced with a knife. While there is no substitute for the pure flavor of butter, you can use a substitute such as margarine in most recipes and they will turn out fairly well.

Sugar Substitute

The best sugar substitute is an all natural product called Zsweet which is available at most health food stores.

Salt

The salt used in this book is Diamond Crystal Kosher Salt. it is half as salty as most other brands. This is because the grains are very fluffy and therefore not as many fit into a measuring spoon. This brand also lists only "salt" as the ingredient on the box. If you are using a different brand than Diamond Crystal Kosher Salt, simply use half the amount specified in the recipe.

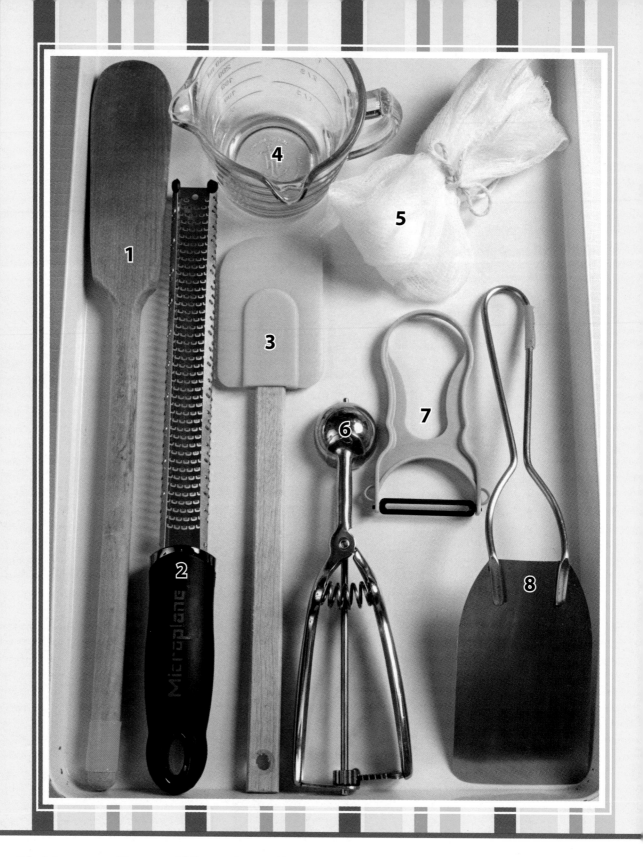

1) Heavy Duty Wooden Spoon

2) Grater

3) Silicone Spatula

4) Glass Measuring Cup

5) Cheesecloth

6) Ice Cream Scoop

7) Peeler

8) Ultra Flexible Spatula

9) **Citrus Juicer**

10) **Nesting Measuring Cup**

11) **Fine Mesh Strainer**

12) **Measuring Spoons**

13) **Coer à la Crème Mold**

14) **Japanese Pastry Brush**

15) **Off Set Spatula**

16) **Craft Scissors**

DRESSINGS & SAUCES

Amish Dressing

Makes 2½ cups

Ingredients

2 cups heavy whipping cream
¼ cup fresh lemon juice
⅓ cup granulated sugar
2 teaspoons kosher salt

An elderly Amish lady gave me this recipe after one of our Quilters' Guild meetings. She said it was the best dressing for first-of-spring vegetables because of its delicate, sweet-tart taste that doesn't overpower the vegetables. Every spring, she serves this dressing with freshly picked baby lettuces from her garden. I love this recipe because of its sheer simplicity and deliciousness. Sometimes, I whisk the dressing more than the recipe calls for to achieve a consistency similar to whipped cream. I love to serve it over sliced avocado and ruby red grapefruit segments.

1. Place all ingredients into a mixing bowl.

2. Using the immersion blender fitted with the whisk attachment, whip for 30 seconds.

3. Taste and adjust the seasoning as desired.

4. Store the dressing covered and refrigerated for up to 5 days.

Marian's Tips:

1) For a variation, add 2 teaspoons of chopped dill or the zest and juice from half of a grapefruit.

2) Make your turkey sandwich extra special by substituting the mayonnaise with this dressing.

3) This dressing is equally good on a tuna salad sandwich. Try it with chopped celery and onion on a poppy seed bagel.

Green Goddess Dressing

Makes 1¼ cups

Ingredients

1 garlic clove

1 packed cup of a mixture of tarragon leaves, parsley sprigs, basil leaves and spinach leaves

1 large egg

2 tablespoons apple cider vinegar

1 anchovy filet

1 teaspoon capers

1 tablespoon granulated sugar

2 teaspoons kosher salt

¼ teaspoon freshly cracked black pepper

1 cup vegetable oil

This dressing is so much better when you make it at home. No bottled dressing can compare to this recipe. The color is gorgeous and it is very versatile in flavor. In addition to being delicious on tossed salads, it is excellent drizzled over seared salmon or chicken breast. It is also superb as a stand-in for mayo on sandwiches and wraps. Once you start making homemade dressings, you won't go back to the grocery store to buy the bottled variety.

Marian's Tip:
I love anchovy in some foods but dislike dealing with those oily little anchovy cans. You can substitute the anchovy filet with 1 teaspoon anchovy paste.

1. Place all ingredients into a tall and narrow container.

2. Position the immersion blender wand at the bottom of the container.

3. Turn the immersion blender on high and blend for 10 seconds at the bottom of the jar.

4. Slowly move the wand up and down while blending until smooth and creamy.

5. Scrape the sides of the container and blend for an additional 10 seconds.

6. Taste and adjust the sugar or seasoning as desired.

7. Store dressing covered and refrigerated for up to 3 days.

Curry Aiöli

Makes 2 cups

Ingredients

2 tablespoons fresh ginger, peeled and sliced

3 tablespoons rice wine vinegar

Zest and juice from 1 lime

1 teaspoon soy sauce

3 garlic cloves

1 tablespoon curry powder

½ teaspoon turmeric

½ jalapeño pepper

1 green onion, chopped

1 tablespoon cilantro leaves

1 tablespoon mint leaves

⅛ cup basil leaves

¼ cup canned sweetened cream of coconut

1 tablespoon kosher salt

1 large egg

1½ cups vegetable oil

Salads, fish, chicken or even fruit, this dressing is delicious on so many different kinds of food. I always keep a container of it in my refrigerator. The ingredient list is a long one, but the immersion blender buzzes them into a creamy and delicious dressing.

1. Place all ingredients into a tall and narrow container.

2. Position the immersion blender wand at the bottom of the container.

3. Turn the immersion blender on high and slowly move the wand up and down while blending until thick and smooth.

4. Store dressing covered and refrigerated for up to 1 week.

Cilantro Mint Dressing

Makes 2 cups

Ingredients

Zest and juice from 2 limes
2 tablespoons soy sauce
2 garlic cloves
¼ cup rice wine vinegar
½ teaspoon sriracha chili sauce
1 bunch cilantro, stems trimmed
1 bunch mint leaves

1 large egg
½ teaspoon kosher salt
Pinch of black pepper
2 tablespoons granulated sugar
2 teaspoons dark sesame oil
1½ cups peanut oil

Wolf serves this dressing on grilled lamb at the restaurant and it's spectacular. The first time I made it, I was skeptical because I saw the huge amount of cilantro and mint going into it. I was pleasantly surprised and really loved it as it was not overpowering and pure magic served on meats. It is also great as a salad dressing. My best friend at the restaurant, Fuji the sushi chef, uses it as a sauce base for pizza. Sauces like this are what differentiates great restaurant food from plain home cooking. Learning a few of Wolf's recipes like this will totally change your food for the better and elevate your cooking skills.

1. Place all ingredients into a tall and narrow container.

2. Position the immersion blender wand at the bottom of the container.

3. Turn the immersion blender on high and slowly move the wand up while blending until the dressing is completely emulsified and finely puréed.

4. Scrape the sides of the container and purée for an additional 20 seconds.

5. Taste and adjust the seasoning as desired.

6. Store dressing covered and refrigerated for up to 1 week.

Marian's Tip:
If you are not a big fan of cilantro, you can substitute it with fresh basil and still have a great tasting dressing.

Russian Dressing

Makes 2 cups

Ingredients

1 tablespoon white vinegar
1 large egg
2 teaspoons kosher salt
1 teaspoon dry mustard powder
⅛ teaspoon cayenne pepper
1 cup vegetable oil

4 tablespoons sweet pickle relish
½ cup ketchup
2 tablespoons barbecue sauce
1 teaspoon Worcestershire sauce
¼ medium red onion, roughly chopped

No other appliance in my kitchen gets more use than my immersion blender, especially for salad dressings. They have to be complex in taste because they get spread over so many greens and vegetables that are quite bland. For that reason, I no longer buy bottled dressings because they always disappoint in taste. The coolest thing about the immersion blender is that it has so much power that it can quickly purée and emulsify any ingredient you throw at it. The ingredient list can be quite long when it comes to dressings but it's easy to just put the ingredients into a container as you measure them and let the immersion blender do the rest.

1. Place all ingredients into the immersion blender beaker.

2. Position the immersion blender wand at the bottom of the container.

3. Turn the immersion blender on high speed while keeping the wand at the bottom for 5 seconds.

4. Slowly move the wand up to emulsify.

5. Taste and adjust the seasoning as desired.

6. Store dressing covered and refrigerated for up to 1 week.

Marian's Tip:
The pickle relish is the secret to this recipe so use a brand you really like.

Sage & Walnut Pesto

Makes 2 cups

Ingredients

½ cup fresh sage leaves
½ cup walnuts, toasted
Zest and juice from ½ of a lemon
1 teaspoon honey
3 garlic cloves
1 teaspoon kosher salt
½ teaspoon freshly ground pepper
¼ cup Parmesan cheese, grated
1 cup walnut or vegetable oil

This pungent pesto is perfect when paired with stronger tasting meats such as lamb or game. I like to spread this mixture over the meat as it roasts to give it a marvelous flavor. Pairing sage with the strong tasting walnuts makes for a delicious tasting sauce. This pesto freezes beautifully so make a big batch and tuck it away in your freezer, ready to add a huge punch of flavor to meat, pasta or even a sandwich.

1. Place all ingredients into the immersion blender chopper bowl.

2. Pulse on high speed until slightly chunky.

3. Store pesto covered and refrigerated for up to 1 week or freeze for up to 3 months.

Marian's Tip:
The walnut oil really adds a great flavor to this recipe. It can be found at most Italian markets. However, if you can't find walnut oil, it will still be delicious using vegetable oil.

Prickly Pear Vinaigrette

Makes 2 cups

Ingredients

2 prickly pears, peeled and quartered
1 garlic clove
2 teaspoons Dijon mustard
2 teaspoons kosher salt
¼ cup granulated sugar
⅓ cup apple cider vinegar
1 large egg
1½ cups vegetable oil

Prickly Pears, also known as Cactus Pears are the pear-shaped fruits that grow on the ends of a variety of cacti. The skins of the fruit are covered with very fine thorns so I peel them using a fork and a pairing knife. They range in color from pale yellow to red but in most markets, they are an incredible scarlet color reminiscent of beets. The flavor is slightly similar to melon. Its sweet and mild flavor makes it perfect for this vinaigrette recipe. Some people strain out the black seeds but I leave them in because I think they are pretty. The season for prickly pears is pretty long, generally from October to May, so try them if you have not already.

1. Place all ingredients into a tall and narrow container.

2. Position the immersion blender wand at the bottom of the container.

3. Turn the immersion blender on high speed while keeping the wand at the bottom for 5 seconds.

4. Slowly move the wand up to emulsify the vinaigrette.

5. Taste and adjust the seasoning as desired.

6. Store vinaigrette covered and refrigerated for up to 1 week.

Marian's Tip:
Use this vinaigrette anywhere you would usually use 1000 Island Dressing.

Brown Butter Vinaigrette

Makes 1 ½ cups

Ingredients

4 tablespoons unsalted butter

1 tablespoon purple onion, chopped

2 teaspoons granulated sugar

2 tablespoons balsamic vinegar

2 tablespoons sherry vinegar

2 teaspoons kosher salt

⅔ cup light olive oil

2 tablespoons real truffle oil (optional)

One of my chef friends gave me this recipe a few years ago. I was intrigued by the butter as it is very unusual to find it in a vinaigrette recipe. Browning the butter before adding it to the other ingredients is pure genius and will make the salad greens really sing. The nutty, tart and slightly sweet flavor will make your mouth very happy. If you can find real truffle oil, it will provide a greater depth to this recipe. It is well worth the extra effort seeking it out. Be sure to serve this vinaigrette warm so that the butter stays in a liquid form.

1. In a saucepan over medium heat, melt the butter for 5 minutes or until it foams and turns brown in color; set aside and let cool.

2. Place the remaining ingredients into a canning jar or container then add the butter.

3. Position the immersion blender wand at the bottom of the jar.

4. Turn the immersion blender on high while keeping the wand at the bottom for 5 seconds.

5. Move the wand up and down to emulsify the vinaigrette.

6. Serve warm or at room temperature.

7. Store the vinaigrette covered and refrigerated for up to 2 weeks.

8. Warm before serving to re-liquify the butter.

Marian's Tip:
For a delicious variation, add an anchovy filet to the ingredients.

Mango Salsa

Makes 2 cups

Ingredients

1 mango, peeled and cut into chunks
¼ medium red onion
3 tablespoons mango nectar
2 tablespoons fresh lime juice
¼ cup cilantro leaves
½ Serrano pepper or as desired
½ teaspoon kosher salt
1 teaspoon granulated sugar

I am fortunate to work with a lovely lady named Estela who is from Hidalgo, Mexico. She speaks very little English, which in turn has greatly improved my Spanish speaking skills. Estela has taught me so much about Mexican food, which is my third favorite cuisine after Chinese and Southern. She has taught me about sauces as well as fresh salsas. Estela will probably give me a big "ai yi yi, jefa" or shake her head when she sees this slightly sweet mango salsa recipe. She would probably not use this fruit or the sugar to make salsa but I really love this recipe. In any case, the secret to great salsa is to make it fresh and at the last minute or the onions get too strong and the flavors become muddy.

1. Place all ingredients into the immersion blender chopper bowl.

2. Pulse until a coarse consistency is achieved.

3. Taste and adjust the seasoning as desired.

4. Serve within 1 hour.

Marian's Tip:
This salsa can be made in advance. Simply keep the ingredients separate and don't combine them until the very last minute.

Corn Salsa

Makes 2 cups

Ingredients

3 ears yellow corn, husks and silk removed
2 Serrano peppers, stems removed
½ medium red onion
¼ red bell pepper, stemmed and seeded
2 tablespoons olive oil
Zest from 1 lime
¼ cup fresh lime juice
2 teaspoons honey

1 teaspoon fresh oregano leaves
3 garlic cloves
Chipotle-flavored hot sauce to taste
A handful of fresh cilantro leaves
½ teaspoon kosher salt

There is a very popular Mexican chain restaurant that I love. Their corn salsa reels me in every time. I think I could make a meal out of just a bowl of corn salsa. I have not been able to exactly replicate their recipe but this one is pretty close.

1. On a grill or grill pan, sear the corn and Serrano peppers on all sides until slightly charred.

2. Let cool slightly.

3. Cut the corn from the cobs into a bowl; set aside.

4. Place remaining ingredients into the immersion blender chopper bowl.

5. Pulse until a coarse consistency is achieved.

6. Transfer the mixture to the bowl holding the corn.

7. Toss well.

8. Taste and adjust the seasoning as desired.

9. Serve immediately.

Marian's Tip:
If you are in a pinch, skip the grilling and use frozen corn kernels. It's not exactly the same but still tastes incredible.

Peach Salsa

Makes 3 cups

Ingredients

1 pound fresh peaches, peeled and pitted

¼ medium red onion, peeled and halved

⅓ cup fresh lime juice

¼ cup peach nectar

1 jalapeño pepper, stems and seeds removed

¼ cup fresh cilantro leaves

½ cup jicama, peeled and diced

⅛ cup fresh basil leaves

2 tablespoons fresh mint leaves

1 garlic clove

½ teaspoon kosher salt

Whenever I make grilled or sautéed fish, I serve it with a fruit salsa like this one. My whole family likes to fish and there is nothing finer than freshly caught fish. The snapper here in St. Petersburg is amazing and often served with fruit salsas at local restaurants. Jicama is a Mexican root that can be found in the Latin section of the grocery store. They are the secret to the crunch in the salsa, which is the perfect juxtaposition to the meltingly tender peaches.

1. Place all ingredients into the immersion blender chopper bowl.

2. Pulse until a coarse consistency is achieved.

3. Taste and adjust the seasoning as desired.

4. Serve within 1 hour.

Marian's Tip:
For a variation, substitute the peaches with a similarly textured and fragrant fruit like apricots or plums.

Estela's Tomato Salsa

Makes 2 cups

Ingredients

4 campari tomatoes
3 plum tomatoes
½ medium white onion
2 Serrano peppers, stems and seeds removed
1 garlic clove
¼ cup cilantro leaves
1 teaspoon kosher salt
1 tablespoon romerito (optional)

Of all the salsas Estela taught me to make, this one is my favorite. She briefly grills some of the vegetables to char them, which adds a great flavor. Estela is from Hidalgo, Mexico. She is a wonderful cook and has a lovely family. Being invited to her home for a meal is both an honor and a joy. She never sits with us as she prefers to be in the kitchen to make sure that we all eat far more than we should. I wish everyone had a friend like Estela.

Marian's Tip:
Romerito is an herb native to Mexico. It looks like fleshy rosemary sprigs. It can be found at Mexican markets. If you can't find it, just omit it as there is no substitute.

1. Preheat a comal, grill pan or sauté pan over medium heat.

2. Add the tomatoes, onions, peppers and garlic to the pan.

3. Grill for 5-10 minutes or until the vegetables are slightly charred; turn once during grilling.

4. Transfer the grilled vegetables to the immersion blender chopper bowl.

5. Chop until a rough consistency is achieved.

6. Add remaining ingredients to the chopper bowl.

7. Pulse until desired consistency and serve.

Green Apple & Curry Salsa

Makes 2 cups

Ingredients

Juice from 1 lemon
⅛ teaspoon cayenne pepper
¼ cup fresh flat leaf parsley
1 teaspoon fresh thyme leaves
1 tablespoon curry powder
1 tablespoon maple syrup
2 tablespoons olive oil
Pinch of kosher salt
Pinch of freshly ground black pepper
2 Granny Smith apples, cored and quartered

This is the salsa I make whenever I fry pork chops for dinner. While pork and apples go very well together, adding the curry and maple syrup makes for a redolent and intoxicating aroma. If you've ever had pork chops with apple sauce, think of this salsa as a grown-up apple sauce with an attitude. I like to serve Sweet Potato Purée with Gingersnap Cookies (see page 119) on the side whenever I serve this dish.

1. Place all ingredients, except apples, into the immersion blender chopper bowl.

2. Pulse until roughly chopped.

3. Add the apples to the chopper bowl and pulse until they are roughly chopped.

4. Serve within 1 hour.

Marian's Tip:
For a variation, try using different types of apples such as Pink Lady, Cox's Orange Pippin, Cortland or Macoun.

SOUPS & MORE

Butternut Squash Soup

Makes 6 servings

Ingredients

2 tablespoons unsalted butter

1 tablespoon olive oil

2 cups yellow onions, chopped

2 pounds butternut squash, peeled, cut into chunks

3 cups chicken stock

2 teaspoons kosher salt

½ teaspoon black pepper

1 cup half & half or whole milk

1 tablespoon honey

2 teaspoons apple cider vinegar

Even though I am a pastry chef, I do not possess a true sweet tooth. I really am a salt person. Whenever I'm asked what I like to cook most, I always answer "homemade soup and great bread". I also believe in cooking once and eating twice. Soups usually taste even better the next day. I do not cook every day but when I do, I make big batches of my favorite foods. Butternut squash falls into that category. I love everything about it, even the happy orange color. This soup is very easy to make. If you have one of the better "U" shaped vegetable peelers (see tools on page 8), you can very easily peel off the squash's skin without having to use a knife.

1. Place the butter and oil into an 8-quart stockpot; let heat until the butter is melted.

2. Add the onions and cook for 5 minutes or until translucent.

3. Reduce the heat to medium-low.

4. Add squash, stock, salt and pepper to the stockpot; let simmer for 30 minutes or until squash is fork tender.

5. Using the immersion blender wand, purée on low speed to avoid splashing.

6. Increase the speed to high and purée until smooth.

7. Add remaining ingredients and purée until combined.

8. Ladle into bowls and serve.

Zellwood Sweet Corn Soup

Makes 5 servings

Ingredients

3 cups yellow onions, chopped

6 tablespoons unsalted butter

¼ cup all purpose flour

1 teaspoon kosher salt

¼ teaspoon turmeric powder

6 cups chicken stock

3 cups Russet potatoes, peeled and diced

5 ears of corn, kernels removed, cobs saved

1 tablespoon granulated sugar

2 teaspoons fresh lemon juice

⅛ teaspoon cayenne pepper

1 cup half & half

Green onions, cut on the bias

Crushed red pepper flakes

My husband Greg grew up in Apopka, Florida which is close to where the Zellwood Sweet Corn Festival is held every summer. His church youth group worked at the festival and Greg has the best memories of driving a tractor to remove giant garbage cans bursting with empty corn cobs after the visitors had eaten their fill of corn. It's always a treat to find Zellwood corn at our local supermarket because it is so sweet and milky. Greg's mom Claire gave me this recipe years ago. She came up with this recipe because of the overabundance of corn during that time of year. She serves it with cornbread made in a family hand-me-down cast iron skillet.

1. In an 8-quart stockpot over medium-high heat, sauté the onions in the butter for 5 minutes or until onions are translucent.

2. Stir in the flour, salt and turmeric; cook for an additional 3 minutes.

3. Add the stock, potatoes and corn kernels to the stockpot; bring to a boil over high heat.

4. Place the corn cobs into the pot for added flavor.

5. Reduce the heat to medium-low and let simmer for 15 minutes or until potatoes are tender.

6. Remove from heat and discard the corn cobs.

7. Using the immersion blender wand, purée on low speed for 5 seconds then increase the speed to high and purée until smooth.

8. Add half & half and blend using the wand until combined.

9. Ladle into bowls, top with remaining ingredients and serve.

Roasted Tomato Basil Soup

Makes 6 servings

Ingredients

3 lbs. ripe plum tomatoes, cut in half lengthwise

¼ cup + 2 tablespoons olive oil, divided

1 tablespoon kosher salt

1½ teaspoons freshly ground black pepper

2 cups yellow onions, chopped

6 garlic cloves, chopped

2 tablespoons unsalted butter

¼ teaspoon crushed red pepper flakes

28 ounces canned plum tomatoes with juice

1 quart chicken stock or water

1 teaspoon fresh thyme leaves

4 cups fresh basil leaves, packed

1. Preheat oven to 400 degrees.

2. In a bowl, combine ripe plum tomatoes, 1/4 cup olive oil, salt and pepper; toss.

3. Place tomatoes in one layer on a baking sheet.

4. Roast in the oven for 45 minutes.

5. Place onions, remaining oil, garlic, butter and red pepper flakes into an 8-quart stockpot over medium heat.

6. Cook for 10 minutes or until onions start to brown.

7. Add remaining ingredients, except basil, to the stockpot.

8. Add the roasted tomatoes and the juice from the baking sheet to the stockpot.

9. Raise the temperature to high and bring to a boil.

10. Lower the heat to medium-low and simmer uncovered for 30 minutes.

11. Using the immersion blender wand, purée on low speed until desire consistency.

12. Ladle into bowls, top with basil and serve.

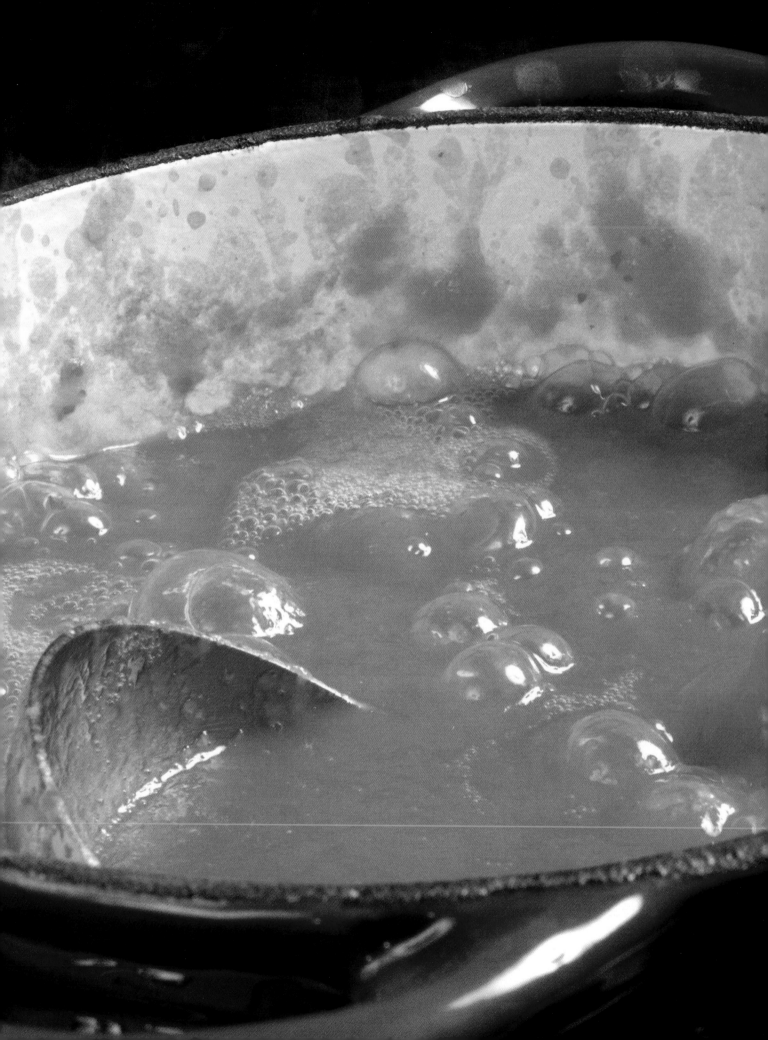

Pea Soup

Makes 6 servings

Ingredients

2 tablespoons unsalted butter

1 medium yellow onion, peeled and quartered

1 teaspoon kosher salt

2 tablespoons all purpose flour

4 cups chicken stock

1 tablespoon granulated sugar

2 teaspoons fresh lemon juice

1½ pounds frozen peas

½ cup plain yogurt

Freshly ground pepper (optional)

If you were given a backstage pass to take a peek inside the freezers of Wolf's restaurants, you might be surprised at what you'd find. You would discover lots of homemade ice creams, some homemade ravioli, items on sheet pans that need quick chilling and always a big box of frozen peas. Frozen peas are the only vegetable I have ever seen in there. When peas are picked off the vine, they start converting their natural sugars into starch. Unless you can get fresh peas from the vine to the table quickly, you are better off using frozen peas. They are grown, harvested, cooked and frozen quickly so that they stay delicious year-round. Add the yogurt to the soup after removing it from the heat or the yogurt will curdle.

1. In a stockpot over medium heat, melt the butter.

2. Add the onions and salt to the stockpot and cook for 5 minutes or until onions are translucent.

3. Stir in the flour; cook for 1 additional minute.

4. Stir in the stock and scrape the bottom of the pot.

5. Bring to a simmer and cook for 5 minutes.

6. Add the sugar, lemon juice and peas.

7. Cook for 10 minutes then remove from heat.

8. Using the immersion blender wand, purée on low speed for 5 seconds then increase the speed to high and purée until smooth.

9. Add the yogurt and pepper to the soup then blend to incorporate.

10. Ladle into bowls and serve.

Potage Parmentier

Makes 6 servings

Ingredients

3 cups Russet potatoes, peeled and diced
3 cups leeks, rinsed and sliced
2 quarts water
1 tablespoon kosher salt
⅓ cup heavy cream
3 tablespoons chives, finely chopped

Although it sounds fancy, Potage Parmentier is just French for potato soup. It is the first soup recipe I ever made out of Julia Child's "Mastering the Art of French Cooking" cookbook. Julia's recipe calls for leeks but we did not have them at all in Africa. I used onions (which Julia says is fine) and I remember it being delicious. We also did not have any nifty electrical appliances so I puréed the soup using an old, cumbersome food mill. Potage Parmentier makes the recipe sound complicated but it is simple and comforting. Six ingredients, a bit of casual cooking and a completely satisfying meal is made. If this soup is puréed until smooth and chilled, it is called Vichyssoise.

1. Place all ingredients, except cream and chives, into an 8-quart stockpot.

2. Bring to a boil over high heat.

3. Reduce the heat to medium and let simmer for 45 minutes or until vegetables are tender.

4. Remove from the stove.

5. Using the immersion blender wand, purée on low speed until desired consistency is achieved.

6. Add the cream to the pot and purée to combine.

7. Ladle into bowls, garnish with chives and serve.

Marian's Tip:
This soup as well as other soups containing potatoes, butternut squash or pumpkin do not freeze well.

Borscht

Makes 6 servings

Ingredients

2 pounds fresh beets, scrubbed

1 yellow onion

6 cups water

¼ cup white vinegar or 2 teaspoons citric acid

¼ cup granulated sugar

2 teaspoons kosher salt

¼ cup heavy cream

¾ cup sour cream

2 tablespoons fresh dill

I love beets! Greg says they taste like dirt but we are both crazy about them. Whenever they are plentiful and cheap at the farmer's market, I buy a big bunch and use them in one of two ways; I either make a stir-fry out of the beet tops and serve it over brown rice or I make this recipe. Occasionally, I add some beef short ribs to the pot but I mostly keep it just vegetables. Borscht is of Russian and Polish origin. It almost always includes a healthy amount of sour cream. Many people boil the beets but the earthy and sweet flavor is much nicer when roasted.

Marian's Tip:
Peeling the beets can stain your hands so wear rubber gloves when removing the peel.

1. Preheat oven to 350 degrees.

2. Place the beets and onion on a baking sheet; bake for 90 minutes.

3. Let cool for 20 minutes.

4. Remove and discard the peel from the beets and onion then cut them into quarters.

5. Place the beets, onions, water, vinegar, sugar and salt into an 8-quart stockpot; bring to a boil then reduce the heat to medium and let simmer for 15 minutes.

6. Remove from heat.

7. Using the immersion blender wand, purée on low for 15 seconds then increase the speed to high and purée until smooth.

8. Add heavy cream and sour cream to the Borscht; purée until combined.

9. Ladle into bowls, garnish with dill and serve.

Creamy Zucchini Soup

Makes 6 servings

Ingredients

1 tablespoon unsalted butter
1 tablespoon olive oil
5 cups leeks, rinsed and chopped
4 cups unpeeled Russet potatoes, rinsed and cubed
4 cups zucchini, chopped
6 cups chicken stock
1 teaspoon kosher salt
½ teaspoon freshly ground black pepper
1 tablespoon fresh lemon juice
2 teaspoons honey
1 teaspoon sriracha hot sauce
½ cup heavy cream
Zucchini ribbons

I make this soup whenever my sweet neighbors leave grocery bags of jumbo-sized zucchini on my door step. I leave jars of homemade bread and jelly on their door step in return. However, I do feel that I am on the better side of the trade-off because I now live in an apartment and cannot grow my own garden.

Marian's Tip:
To make the zucchini ribbons, use a mandoline slicer or vegetable peeler.

1. Place butter and oil into an 8-quart stockpot over medium-low heat; let butter melt.

2. Add leeks to the stockpot and sauté for 5 minutes.

3. Add potatoes, zucchini, stock, salt and pepper to the stockpot.

4. Bring to a boil then reduce the temperature to medium heat and let simmer for 30 minutes.

5. Using the immersion blender wand, purée on low speed until smooth.

6. Add lemon juice, honey, sriracha and heavy cream to the soup; purée until combined.

7. Ladle into bowls, garnish with zucchini ribbons and serve.

Salt Cod Fritters

Makes 20 small fritters

Ingredients

1 pound dried, boneless salt cod

2 cups whole milk

5 garlic cloves, divided

2 bay leaves

5 sprigs fresh thyme

4 large Russet potatoes, peeled and quartered

1 large onion, quartered

½ cup fresh flat leaf parsley

½ cup fresh cilantro

2 large eggs

Peanut oil

Kosher salt to taste

Freshly ground black pepper to taste

Lemon wedges

1. Soak the cod in water for 24 hours, changing the water 3 times to remove the salt.

2. Drain, rinse and transfer the cod to a stockpot.

3. Add milk, 3 garlic cloves, bay leaves and thyme to the stockpot; add enough water to cover the pot contents by 1 inch.

4. Bring to a boil then reduce the heat to medium-low and let simmer for 20 minutes or until the cod is tender; drain, discard the milk and set aside.

5. In a separate stockpot, combine potatoes and enough water to cover them; bring to a simmer over medium heat and cook for 20 minutes or until the potatoes are tender then drain and set aside.

6. Add the cod, onions, remaining garlic cloves, parsley, cilantro and eggs to the chopper bowl; pulse to combine but still chunky.

7. Coarsely mash the potatoes using a fork and add chopper bowl contents to the stockpot; stir to combine.

8. In a large pot, heat 1 inch of peanut oil until the temperature is 370 degrees on a thermometer.

9. Using a small ice cream scoop, shape the mixture then drop them into the oil and fry for 2-3 minutes or until brown on all sides (turn once during frying).

10. Drain on paper towels, add salt and pepper if needed then serve with lemon wedges.

Southern Deviled Eggs

Makes 16 eggs

Ingredients

12 large eggs
½ cup mayonnaise (see page 126)
2 teaspoons yellow mustard
2 tablespoons sweet pickle relish
1 teaspoon kosher salt

½ teaspoon granulated sugar
⅛ teaspoon cayenne pepper
2 teaspoons cider vinegar
Paprika for sprinkling

1. Place eggs and enough water to cover the eggs by 1 inch into a stockpot.

2. Bring to a boil over high heat.

3. As soon as the water starts to boil, reduce the heat to low and cook for exactly 10 minutes.

4. Remove from heat and add cold water to the pot to slightly cool the eggs.

5. Crack each egg multiple times against the side of the pot.

6. Peel the eggs under a hard stream of cold water from the faucet.

7. Place the eggs into a bowl of cold water and let cool for 10 minutes.

8. Cut eggs in half lengthwise, remove the egg yolks and place the yolks into the immersion blender chopper bowl.

9. Rinse the egg white halves, wrap them in plastic wrap and chill until ready to use.

10. Add remaining ingredients, except paprika to the egg yolks in the chopper bowl.

11. Blend until smooth.

12. Taste and adjust the seasoning as desired.

13. Transfer egg mixture to a pastry bag and pipe mixture into the egg white halves.

14. Sprinkle with paprika then cover and chill until ready to serve.

Chicken Salad

Makes 4 servings

Ingredients

½ celery stalk

¼ medium red onion

¼ cup walnuts, toasted

¼ Golden Delicious apple, cored and quartered

3 cups cooked chicken, skin removed and de-boned

¼ cup raisins

¼ cup red seedless grapes

2 tablespoons sweet relish

½ cup mayonnaise (see page 126)

1 tablespoon yellow mustard

1 teaspoon kosher salt

½ teaspoon freshly ground pepper

½ teaspoon lemon juice

½ teaspoon celery seeds

1 teaspoon hot sauce

I think this recipe should really be called "Fruited Chicken Salad". It has almost as much fruit in it as anything else, which is exactly how I like it. It is a flavor and texture explosion, where each bite has a different taste and crunch so it never gets boring. I like to serve this salad as an informal supper on really soft homemade rolls. This is a great recipe to make with leftover rotisserie chicken.

Marian's Tip:
After Thanksgiving, I make this with leftover turkey and fold in a handful of stuffing to add a great herb flavor.

1. Place the celery, onions, walnuts and apple into the immersion blender chopper bowl.

2. Pulse 3 times or until a chunky consistency is achieved.

3. Transfer the mixture to a large bowl.

4. Place the chicken into the immersion blender chopper bowl and pulse to desired texture.

5. Transfer the chicken to the bowl holding the onion mixture.

6. Place remaining ingredients into the immersion blender chopper bowl and pulse to combine.

7. Transfer the mixture to the bowl holding the chicken and onion mixture; toss using a spoon and serve.

8. Store chicken salad covered and refrigerated for up to 2 days.

Chipotle White Bean Dip

Makes 2 cups

Ingredients

1 can (15.5 ounces) cannellini beans, drained
2 garlic cloves
1 teaspoon fresh lime zest
Juice from 1 lime
1 teaspoon Adobo all purpose seasoning
1 green onion, chopped

1 teaspoon soy sauce
4 tablespoons chipotles en adobo
1 teaspoon honey
2 tablespoons tomato paste
2 tablespoons vegetable oil

One day, I wanted to make hummus and discovered that I did not have any chickpeas, which are the beans most associated with hummus. I made it anyway using a can of cannellini beans I found in my pantry. I added some chipotles en adobo, which is a delightful Mexican concoction of smoked jalapeño peppers in a flavorful tomato sauce (it is sold in small cans). I am addicted to that stuff and sneak it into many of my sauces and soups. It is pretty spicy so use less if you are not used to spicy foods. My family now prefers this dip over any other version and I think you will like it as well. The ingredient list is a little long but the immersion blender does all the work.

1. Place all ingredients into the immersion blender chopper bowl.

2. Purée for 30 seconds or until smooth.

3. Scrape the sides of the chopper bowl and purée for an additional 30 seconds.

4. Taste and adjust the seasoning as desired.

5. Store dip covered and refrigerated for up to 2 weeks.

SHAKES, SMOOTHIES & DRINKS

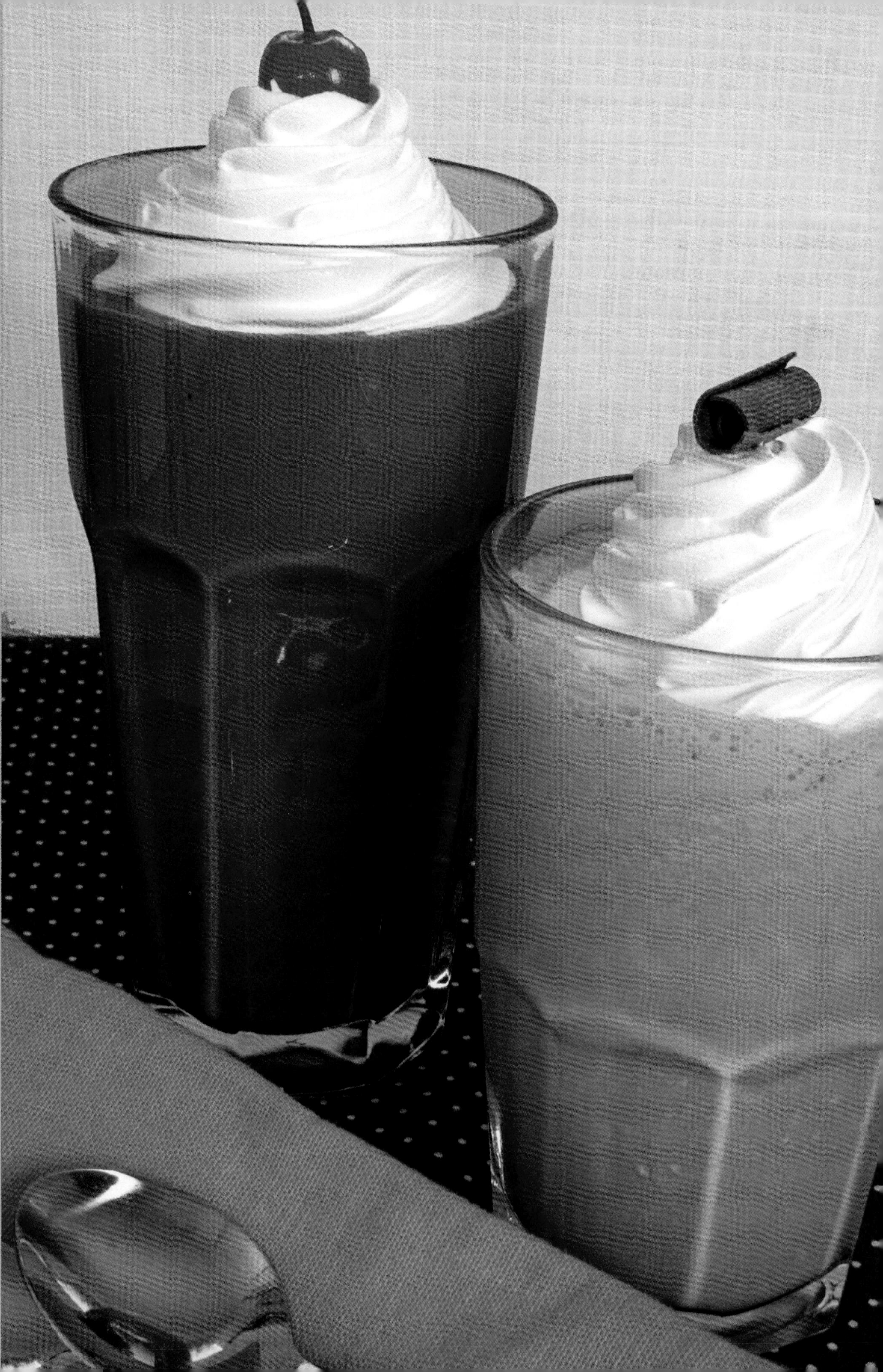

Chocolate & Coffee Milk Shakes

Makes 2 servings

Chocolate Milk Shake

4 scoops vanilla ice cream
½ cup chocolate ganache (see page 130)
½ cup half & half

Coffee Milk Shake

4 scoops vanilla ice cream
½ cup half & half
¼ cup strong coffee, cold
2 teaspoons instant espresso powder

The reason there are two recipes on this page is that in my family, we are divided on which milk shake tastes better. Greg and Jordan prefer the coffee milk shake, Ben and I like the chocolate one better. Whenever we make milk shakes, we just make both and layer them into pretty glasses.

1. Place all chocolate milk shake ingredients into the immersion blender chopper bowl.

2. Pulse until smooth.

3. Fill each glass halfway with chocolate milk shake.

4. Rinse out the chopper bowl.

5. Place all coffee milk shake ingredients into the immersion blender chopper bowl.

6. Pulse until smooth.

7. Top off each glass with coffee milk shake and serve.

Marian's Tip:
You can find instant espresso powder in the coffee aisle at most grocery stores.

Old Fashioned Strawberry Milk Shake

Makes 2 servings

Ingredients

1 cup strawberries, cut in half
¼ cup granulated sugar
4 scoops strawberry ice cream
⅓ cup half & half

Whipped Topping

1 cup heavy cream
2 tablespoons granulated sugar

People don't make milk shakes like this anymore. I think it's because you need a little patience and we are all too busy these days to make time-consuming recipes. Really though, stirring some sugar into strawberries and then waiting for the sugar to work its magic is hardly difficult to do. This process is called macerating. The sugar breaks down the cells of the strawberries enough to pull the juices out of them. The juice becomes intensely flavored from the softened berries which become more mellow in taste. It's just delicious.

1. Place strawberries and sugar into a bowl; toss.

2. Cover and let strawberries macerate at room temperature for 30 minutes.

3. Transfer the strawberries and their juice to a pitcher.

4. Using the immersion blender wand, purée until a rough consistency is achieved.

5. Add the ice cream and half & half to the pitcher.

6. Blend using the wand until well combined.

7. Divide between glasses.

8. In a bowl, combine topping ingredients.

9. Using the immersion blender fitted with the whisk attachment, whisk on high speed until soft peaks form.

10. Top each milk shake with a spoonful of whipped topping, garnish with a whole strawberry and serve.

Strawberry Kiwi Kooler

Makes 2 servings

Ingredients

6 whole strawberries, tops removed
3 tablespoons granulated sugar, divided
6 kiwi, peeled
1 cup pear nectar
1 cup ice

Kiwi fruits are indigenous to the Yangtze River basin in China. It is locally known as sun peach, monkey peach and macaque (French for monkey) peach. The fruit reached its now more common home of New Zealand through missionaries at the turn of the last century. In New Zealand, the kiwi is also called Chinese gooseberry because in the early days, people boiled the kiwi which made it taste similar to gooseberry. They were unaware that kiwi could be eaten raw, which is much more delicious. Today the fruit is eaten almost exclusively raw and is available year round.

1. Place the strawberries and 1 tablespoon sugar into the immersion beaker.

2. Using the immersion blender wand, pulse on high speed until smooth.

3. Divide mixture between the serving glasses.

4. Place remaining ingredients into the immersion blender chopper bowl.

5. Pulse on high speed until smooth.

6. Pour over the strawberries into the glasses and serve.

Citrus Slushy

Makes 2 servings

Ingredients

1 cup orange juice, freshly squeezed
¼ orange with skin (optional)
¼ cup grapefruit juice, freshly squeezed
1 tablespoon lemon juice, freshly squeezed
1 tablespoon granulated sugar
1½ cups ice cubes
8 Mandarin orange segments, divided
2 lime wedges

I find this to be one of the best ways to start a perfect Florida day. The orange with skin adds a heady aroma and taste from the natural oils found in the skin. It will not taste bitter if you don't add more than ¼ of the orange's skin. I often make these slushies and pack the mixture into hollowed out orange halves then freeze them to always have a healthy dessert on hand.

1. Place all ingredients, except orange segments and lime wedges, into the immersion blender chopper bowl.

2. Blend until smooth.

3. If you prefer a thicker slushy, add some ice cubes and blend again.

4. Drop 4 Mandarin orange segments into the bottom of each glass.

5. Divide the slushy between the glasses.

6. Garnish each glass with a lime wedge.

7. Serve immediately.

BREADS & QUICK BREADS

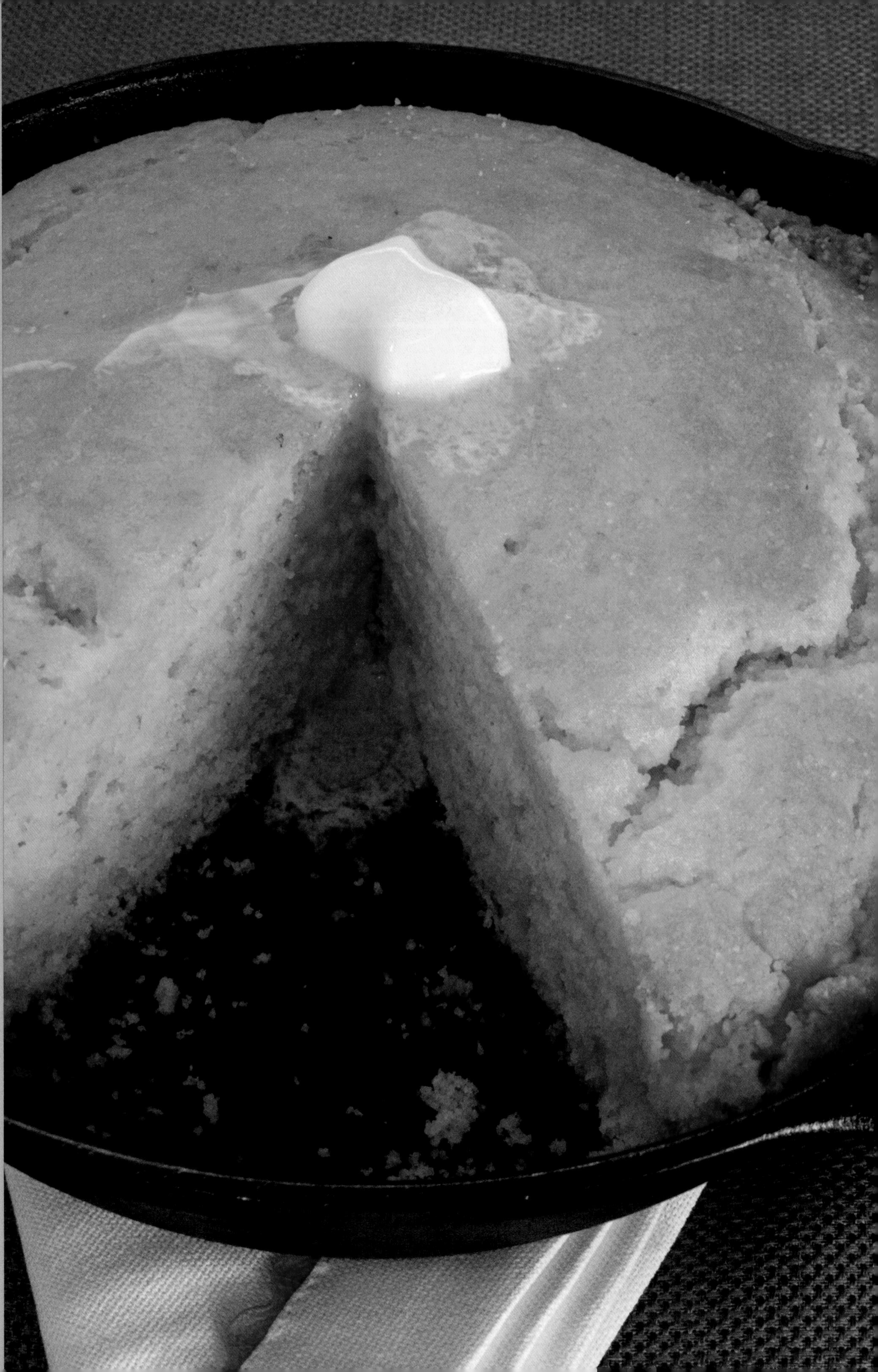

Cast Iron Skillet Cornbread

Makes 6 - 8 servings

Ingredients

2¼ cups yellow cornmeal
⅓ cup unsalted butter, melted
1 tablespoon granulated sugar
1 teaspoon baking soda

1 teaspoon baking powder
1 teaspoon kosher salt
2 large eggs
2 tablespoons additional unsalted butter for the skillet

In one of Jacque Pepin's cookbooks, I learned his secret of toasting cornmeal before using it in a recipe. It is the most extraordinary way to add a huge boost of corn flavor to this cornbread recipe. It is such a simple step yet such a revelation in taste. I now use his method with many grains such as cornmeal, oats or even flour.

Marian's Tip:
To change it up, fold in some diced bell peppers, jalapeno peppers, shredded cheddar cheese, green onions, corn kernels or hot dogs after step 7.

1. Preheat oven to 400 degrees.

2. Spread the cornmeal out on a cookie sheet.

3. Bake for 8-10 minutes or until brown and nutty smelling.

4. Remove and let cool.

5. Place a 10-inch cast iron skillet in the oven and keep the temperature at 400 degrees.

6. In a bowl, combine cornmeal and remaining ingredients, except the butter for the skillet.

7. Using the immersion blender fitted with the whisk attachment, whisk until smooth.

8. Open the oven door and carefully add the remaining butter to the cast iron skillet.

9. Once the butter has melted, carefully pour the batter into the cast iron skillet.

10. Bake for 15-18 minutes or until golden brown.

11. Serve hot.

Hurry Up Biscuits

Makes 8 biscuits

Ingredients

1½ cups all purpose flour
1 tablespoon granulated sugar
2 teaspoons baking powder
½ teaspoon kosher salt
1 cup heavy cream
Additional heavy cream and sugar for tops (optional)

I love this simple stir-together recipe because it tastes fantastic. These biscuits get all the moisture and fat they need from the cream, thus eliminating having to cut fat into the flour which is common in most biscuit recipes. It is a treasure to have a simple and quick recipe like this in my files because there are so many other tasks in the kitchen that take alot of time and effort. Enjoy them plain as biscuits or add dried fruit, nuts, chocolate, cheese or herbs. You can also brush the tops with additional cream and turn them into scones. They also make fantastic dumplings by dropping the raw dough onto bubbling stews. In addition, they make a nice topping for fruit cobblers sprinkled with a bit of additional sugar.

1. Preheat oven to 375 degrees.

2. Line a cookie sheet with parchment paper.

3. Place all ingredients into the immersion blender chopper bowl.

4. Pulse until a dough ball forms.

5. Using a small ice cream scoop, drop biscuits onto the cookie sheet.

6. Pat down the top of each biscuit using your finger.

7. If desired, brush cream on each biscuit and top with additional sugar.

8. Bake for 15-20 minutes or until golden brown and puffed.

9. Serve hot.

Greg's Favorite Dinner Rolls

Makes 8 rolls

Ingredients

1½ cups bread flour
¼ cup powdered milk
1 teaspoon kosher salt
1 tablespoon granulated sugar

1 package active dry yeast
1 large egg
2 tablespoons unsalted butter, melted
⅔ cup water, room temperature

In my home, dinner rolls are preferred over biscuits, cornbread or any other form of bread. I came up with this recipe for Greg's birthday this year and he says that they are the best rolls I have ever made for him. My son Ben was home for the birthday dinner and he had to fight Greg for the last roll. Whenever I serve these rolls, the men in my family have the amusing habit of turning whatever foods I have prepared into little sandwiches. When making a bread dough, I like to include powdered milk in the recipe because it significantly improves the flavor, texture, softness and rise.

Marian's Tip:
If you prefer your rolls to have softer sides, place them on the baking tray so they almost touch each other. If you prefer brown sides, place them 2 inches apart.

1. Place all ingredients into the immersion blender chopper bowl.

2. Pulse on low for 30 seconds or until a smooth dough ball forms.

3. Let the dough rest for 10 minutes inside the covered chopper bowl.

4. Mix continuously for an additional 30 seconds.

5. Shape the dough into 8 rolls.

6. Place the rolls on a parchment-lined baking tray.

7. Cover rolls with a cloth and let rise for 40 minutes.

8. Preheat oven to 350 degrees.

9. Bake for 20 minutes or until brown and well risen.

10. Serve hot.

Pistachio Crusted French Toast

Makes 4 servings

Ingredients

1½ cups pistachio nuts, divided
6 large eggs
½ teaspoon pure vanilla extract
2 cups heavy cream
1 loaf brioche or challah bread, hand sliced into 8 thick slices
Butter
Maple syrup
Powdered sugar

Pistachio Crusted French Toast is one of the most decadent breakfast dishes I know. The recipe is a Wolfgang Puck creation that is to die for. It is easy to make and an impressive dish to serve. You can assemble all of the components the day before however the sautéing has to be done right before serving. Use the gorgeous green Sicilian pistachio nuts if they are available at your market.

Marian's Tip:
This recipe can be prepared with other nuts such as chopped macadamia nuts or pecans.

1. Place half of the nuts into the immersion blender chopper bowl.

2. Pulse until coarsely ground, remove and repeat with remaining nuts; transfer nuts to a shallow plate and set aside.

3. In a bowl, combine eggs, vanilla and cream.

4. Using the immersion blender fitted with the whisk attachment, whisk until smooth.

5. Pour mixture into a shallow bowl.

6. Preheat a large sauté pan over medium heat.

7. Dip bread slices on both sides into the egg mixture then dip one side of each slice into the ground pistachio nuts.

8. Apply non-stick spray to the sauté pan.

9. Place bread slices, nut-side up into the pan and cook for 3 minutes or until golden brown. Flip and cook for 2 minutes then serve topped with butter, syrup and/or powdered sugar.

Individual Yorkshire Puddings

Makes 6 puddings

Ingredients

¾ cup whole milk
3 large eggs
1 tablespoon fresh chives, snipped
¾ teaspoon kosher salt
¾ cup all purpose flour
6 teaspoons lard or bacon grease, divided

Yorkshire puddings are usually made in a large pan, but they are darling when made into individual mini puddings. They are traditionally served with roast beef and gravy. My mom used to make it in a 9x13-inch pan and served it cut into squares. The English call all sorts of foods "puddings" that Americans would not consider them to be. This dish tastes somewhere between bread, pancakes and crêpes yet is plain enough that almost everyone likes it. When they are finished baking, they have a crispy and puffed top with a moist and somewhat creamy interior. Simply delicious.

Marian's Tip:
If you have a cast iron muffin tin, your Yorkshire puddings will be especially crispy and delightful.

1. Preheat oven to 400 degrees.

2. Move a rack to the lower part of the oven and place an empty cookie sheet on the rack to catch drippings.

3. Place all ingredients, except lard, into a pitcher.

4. Using the immersion blender wand, mix until a thin batter is achieved.

5. Drop 1 teaspoon of lard into each well of a 6 cup muffin tin.

6. Place the muffin tin on the center rack of the oven and heat for 5 minutes.

7. Open the oven door and carefully fill each muffin well with batter until 2/3 full.

8. Bake for 30 minutes or until the puddings have risen a few inches above the pan and are deep brown in color.

9. Serve immediately before they deflate.

Sam's Pancakes

Makes 12 pancakes

Ingredients

⅓ cup sour cream

2 cups buttermilk

3 large eggs

2 cups unbleached all purpose flour

1 teaspoon kosher salt

2 tablespoons granulated sugar

½ teaspoon baking soda

1 teaspoon baking powder

Unsalted Butter

Maple syrup

In the Old Port Tampa area, Greg's Dad Sam had the reputation for making the best pancakes. He achieved that status with this delicious recipe. Sam served them up by the hundreds at their Methodist Church fundraiser pancake breakfasts. He told me the secret is using plenty of tangy buttermilk and a bit of sour cream. Also, the batter needs to be mixed very quickly and not for too long. He said that if little lumps remain in the finished batter, it is a sure sign that the pancakes will be fluffy. He was right.

1. Preheat an electric griddle or sauté pan to 350 degrees.

2. In a large bowl, combine sour cream, buttermilk and eggs.

3. Using the immersion blender fitted with the whisk attachment, whisk on low speed until just combined.

4. Add remaining ingredients, except butter and syrup.

5. Quickly whisk on low speed to incorporate (leave some lumps to ensure that the pancakes will be fluffy).

6. Let rest for 5 minutes.

7. Ladle the batter on the griddle and cook for 2 minutes on each side or until brown.

8. Serve topped with butter and syrup.

Sage & Red Onion Focaccia

Makes 4 - 6 servings

Dough Ingredients

½ cup + 2 tablespoons water, room temperature
1 envelope dry active yeast
2 tablespoons honey
1½ cups all purpose flour
1 teaspoon kosher salt
1 tablespoon vegetable oil
2 tablespoons unsalted butter, melted

Toppings

1 teaspoon kosher salt
2 tablespoons fresh sage leaves, torn
¼ red onion, thinly sliced

Focaccia bread is one of the easier doughs to make. Using the immersion blender chopper bowl makes it extra fast and easy. The dough is very wet, almost pourable, which contributes to all the irregular shaped holes found in classic focaccia bread. The toppings I have chosen are not really Italian but I find the combination of butter, red onion and sage to be irresistible. This is my go-to bread recipe to serve alongside a perfect roasted chicken and vegetables.

1. Place all dough ingredients, except butter into the immersion blender chopper bowl.

2. Blend on medium speed for 30 seconds or until a smooth and wet dough forms.

3. Let rest for 10 minutes then blend again for 10 seconds.

4. Pour half of the butter onto a small sheet pan and spread it around the pan.

5. Pour the dough onto the pan and top with remaining butter.

6. Pat and pull dough to fit the shape of the pan then let it rest for 30 minutes.

7. Preheat oven to 400 degrees.

8. Dimple the dough all over with your fingers then let it rest for 5 minutes.

9. Top with topping ingredients and bake for 20 minutes or until puffed and brown (rotate pan halfway after 10 minutes of baking).

10. Serve hot cut into wedges.

Whole Wheat Flatbread Crackers

Makes 6 flatbreads

Dough Ingredients

1 cup all purpose flour
½ cup 100% whole wheat flour
1 teaspoon kosher salt
⅔ cup water

Toppings

Olive oil
Parmesan cheese, grated
Red onion, thinly sliced
Fresh thyme or other herbs
Kosher salt
Freshly cracked pepper
Crushed red pepper flakes

At Spago, each bread basket presented to guests is filled with a variety of artisan breads as well as this flatbread. It is crunchy, earthy, flavorful and completely addicting. You can turn this recipe into pizzas by changing the toppings and cheeses but if you like yours crispy, go easy on the toppings.

1. Preheat oven to 450 degrees.

2. Place the dough ingredients into the immersion blender chopper bowl.

3. Pulse on high speed until a dough ball forms.

4. Divide the dough into 6 balls.

5. Using a floured rolling pin, roll each ball out as flat as possible.

6. Divide flatbreads between 2 cookie sheets.

7. Brush flatbreads with olive oil and sprinkle with desired toppings (do not put too many toppings on the flatbreads or they won't be crispy.)

8. Bake for 7-10 minutes or until well browned.

9. Top with additional herbs, salt and a drizzle of olive oil before serving.

Whole Wheat Pizza Dough

Makes 1 pizza crust

Ingredients

⅔ cup water
1 tablespoon olive oil
1 tablespoon honey
1½ teaspoons kosher salt
1½ cups 100% whole wheat flour
1 package active dry yeast
1 teaspoon onion powder (optional)
1 teaspoon Italian seasoning (optional)

This is the whole wheat version of Wolf's famous pizza dough. It is the best whole wheat crust I have ever tasted and it is good enough that you won't miss the white flour crust ever again. The dough freezes well so I always have a stash of dough balls in my freezer for a quick pizza, flatbread or calzone. Whole wheat flour contains bran, germ and endosperm (all of the good-for-you parts) which can go rancid quite quickly. For this reason, I store my whole wheat flour in the freezer.

1. Place all ingredients into the immersion blender chopper bowl.

2. Mix on high speed for 30 seconds or until a dough ball forms.

3. Let rest for 10 minutes then mix for an additional 30 seconds.

4. Shape dough into a smooth ball.

5. On a lightly floured surface, pat dough into a flat disk; cover and let rest for 30 minutes.

6. Preheat oven to 450 degrees.

7. Stretch the dough into a pizza shape and top with desired toppings.

8. Bake for 10-15 minutes or until well browned and serve.

Marian's Tip:
For 1 pizza, use about 2 tablespoons of sauce and 2/3 cup of shredded cheese. Any more will prevent the crust from cooking well and it won't get crispy.

Chocolate Crinkle Cookies

Makes 24 cookies

Ingredients

1 cup semi-sweet chocolate chips, melted, slightly cooled
2½ cups granulated sugar
1½ teaspoons baking powder
½ teaspoon kosher salt
⅓ cup vegetable oil
2 large eggs

1 large egg yolk
2 tablespoons light corn syrup
1 tablespoon vanilla extract
1¾ cups all purpose flour
Granulated sugar for rolling
Powdered sugar for rolling

1. Place all ingredients, except flour and sugars for rolling, into the immersion blender chopper bowl.

2. Mix on medium speed until smooth.

3. Remove the blade and stir in the flour using a rubber spatula.

4. Scrape the sides of the bowl and mix for an additional 5 seconds.

5. Transfer the dough to a covered container and chill for at least 3 hours.

6. Preheat oven to 325 degrees.

7. Line 2 cookie sheets with parchment paper.

8. Use a small ice cream scoop to form even balls of dough.

9. Roll each ball between your hands to make them round.

10. Roll each ball in granulated sugar then in powdered sugar.

11. Space the balls out evenly on the cookie sheets.

12. Bake for 15 minutes or until puffed and crackled.

13. Remove and serve warm.

Raspberry or Chocolate Mousse

Makes 4 - 6 servings

Raspberry Mousse

1½ cups heavy cream
1 tablespoon granulated sugar
½ cup Raspberry Coulis (see page 128)

Chocolate Mousse

1½ cups heavy cream
1 tablespoon granulated sugar
¼ teaspoon vanilla extract
½ cup chocolate ganache (see page 130)

When we make these mousse recipes on HSN, we call them "Mousse-in-a-Minute". It literally takes less than a minute to make them. The taste is decadent and will have your family thinking that you spent far more time making it. I like to serve these with store bought pirouette cookies, which are long and rolled up like a thin cigarette with chocolate in the middle.

1. Place all Raspberry Mousse or Chocolate Mousse ingredients into the immersion blender beaker.

2. Using the immersion blender fitted with the whisk attachment, whisk until smooth and stiff peaks form.

3. Divide mousse between parfait glasses.

4. Serve immediately.

Marian's Tips:
Make sure the chocolate ganache is still pourable but not hot or it will take a long time for the cream to thicken.

Butter Cake with Berry Icing

Makes 8 - 10 servings

Cake Ingredients

¾ cup unsalted butter, melted and cooled
1 tablespoon baking powder
1¾ cups granulated sugar
1 teaspoon kosher salt
2 teaspoons vanilla extract
5 large egg whites
2¾ cups cake flour, divided
1 cup whole milk, divided

Fruit Ingredients

Juice from ½ lemon
¼ cup granulated sugar
1 vanilla bean, split and scraped
1 pint strawberries, hulled and halved
1 pint raspberries

Icing

Swiss Meringue (see page 136)

1. Preheat oven to 350 degrees; grease and flour a jelly roll pan then set aside.

2. In a bowl, combine butter, baking powder, sugar, salt and vanilla.

3. Using the immersion blender fitted with the whisk attachment, cream the bowl contents on low speed for 1 minute or until light and fluffy.

4. Scrape the bowl then continue to mix while adding the egg whites until combined.

5. Remove the blade and fold in the flour and milk using a rubber spatula.

6. Pour the batter into the jelly roll pan then bake for 20-25 minutes (test for doneness using a toothpick).

7. Let cool then chill for 1 hour or until cold.

8. In a saucepan over medium heat, combine lemon juice, sugar and vanilla bean; stir constantly until sugar is dissolved then add the berries. Remove and let cool.

9. In a bowl, blend 1/4 cup of fruit mixture using the immersion blender wand until a rough consistency is achieved. Add Swiss Meringue to the bowl and fold it in using a rubber spatula so that the icing remains very streaky.

10. To assemble the cake, remove chilled cake from the pan and cut it into 3 equal rectangles. Ice each rectangle top and stack. Ice the cake's top and sides, top with remaining fruit and serve.

Chocolate Baby Cakes

Makes 12 servings

Baby Cake Ingredients

2 cups semi-sweet chocolate chips

1¼ cups unsalted butter

2 teaspoons instant espresso powder (optional)

8 large eggs

1 cup granulated sugar

¼ cup all purpose flour

Vanilla Icing

3 cups powdered sugar

¼ teaspoon almond extract

¼ teaspoon butter-vanilla extract

½ teaspoon vanilla extract

¼ teaspoon kosher salt

1 cup unsalted butter, softened

3 large egg whites

Baby cake is the whimsical name for a cake that is shaped like a mini loaf instead of a cupcake. The pan used to make them is identical to a muffin or cupcake pan except that the wells are small rectangles instead of rounds.

Marian's Tips:
Although it is unusual to fill the pan almost to the top, the baby cakes don't rise much.
If you like a chocolate on chocolate variation, ice the tops with the chocolate ganache on page 130.

1. Preheat oven to 325 degrees and grease a baby cake pan.

2. In a microwave-safe bowl, combine the chocolate chips, butter and espresso; microwave for 3 minutes or until chocolate has melted.

3. Place the eggs and sugar into a large bowl.

4. Using the immersion blender fitted with the whisk attachment, mix on high for 2 minutes or until the mixture is fluffy and pale yellow in color.

5. Using a spatula, fold the flour as well as the chocolate mixture into the egg mixture until combined.

6. Pour the batter into the baby cake pan until each well is almost filled to the top then bake for 25-30 minutes or until tops look dry.

7. In the bowl of a stand mixer fitted with the beaters, combine all icing ingredients; whip on high speed for 5 minutes or until fluffy.

8. Spread the icing over the cooled cakes and serve.

Strawberry Rhubarb Bavarian Cream

Makes 6 servings

Ingredients

2 cups rhubarb, chopped
2 cups strawberries, hulled
1¼ cups granulated sugar
2 envelopes (¼ ounce size each) unflavored gelatin
¼ cup water
3 large egg whites
2 cups heavy cream

Strawberries and rhubarb have a natural affinity for each other and this stunning dessert is the perfect way to showcase that attraction. The word "Bavarian" makes this recipe sound fancy, but it is really easy to put together. The name would seem to indicate that the recipe is of German origin but that is not the case. No one seems to know exactly who thought of this delightful concoction first but the French named this dessert Bavarois.

1. Apply non-stick spray to a decorative mold or cake pan; set aside.

2. In a microwave-safe bowl, combine rhubarb, strawberries and sugar; microwave for 6 minutes or until rhubarb has softened.

3. In a small bowl, combine gelatin and water; stir quickly and let rest for 5 minutes.

4. Add the gelatin mixture to the hot rhubarb mixture and stir until the gelatin has dissolved. Chill mixture until semi solid.

5. Using the immersion blender fitted with the whisk attachment, whisk egg whites in a bowl until soft peaks form and the tips curl over.

6. In a separate bowl, whisk the cream on high speed until soft peaks form.

7. Using a silicone spatula, gently fold all three mixtures together, spoon it into the mold or cake pan and chill for 3 hours or until set.

8. Invert onto a serving plate and serve.

Classic Bundt Cake with Pear Chips

Makes 1 cake

Cake Ingredients

1½ cups unsalted butter, melted then cooled
1½ cups granulated sugar
1 teaspoon kosher salt
1 teaspoon vanilla extract
6 large eggs
2 cups all purpose flour
½ cup pear-flavored mini jelly beans
1 firm Bosc pear

Glaze

½ cup powdered sugar
3 tablespoons whole milk

1. Preheat oven to 325 degrees; apply non-stick spray to a Bundt cake or tube pan.

2. Place butter, sugar, salt and vanilla into the immersion blender chopper bowl.

3. Mix on high for 30 seconds, scrape the bowl then mix for an additional 10 seconds.

4. Add the eggs to the chopper bowl and mix for an additional 30 seconds.

5. Remove the blade and stir in the flour and jelly beans using a rubber spatula.

6. Pour the batter into the prepared pan.

7. Bake for 1 hour (test for doneness using a toothpick); let cool completely.

8. Using a mandoline, slice the pear lengthwise into very thin slices.

9. Line a cookie sheet with parchment paper and place the pear slices on it.

10. Bake the pear slices at 200 degrees for 2 hours or until dry and brittle; let cool.

11. In a bowl, combine glaze ingredients; mix well.

12. Unmold the cake, drizzle it with glaze, decorate it with pear chips and serve.

Chocolate Sorbet

Makes 4 servings

Ingredients

3 cups ice cubes
½ cup chocolate ganache (see page 130)
1 teaspoon instant espresso powder

It is hard to believe that 3 little ingredients can make such a smooth, refreshing and satisfying sorbet. It tastes like a cross between ice cream and Italian ice. The immersion blender is great at turning ice cubes into "snow", which makes the texture so incredible. This recipe is Wolf's own creation. One day, he wanted ice cream but I did not have any at the studio. He started adding ingredients to the immersion blender and out came this recipe. Now we make it all the time for a quick pick-me-up.

1. Place all ingredients into the immersion blender chopper bowl.

2. Pulse until smooth.

3. Scrape the sides of the chopper bowl then pulse again.

4. If any ice cube pieces remain, remove them.

5. Scoop sorbet into pretty serving dishes.

6. Serve immediately.

Coeur à la Crème

Makes 6 servings

Ingredients

2½ cups heavy cream

2 teaspoons pure vanilla extract

¼ teaspoon lemon zest

Seeds scraped from 1 vanilla bean

12 ounces cream cheese, room temperature

1¼ cups powdered sugar

Raspberry Coulis (see page 128)

1 pint fresh raspberries

When I was pastry chef for Wolf at his café in Orlando, this was a favorite way for would-be grooms to propose. In the pastry department, we would suspend the engagement ring in a nest of spun sugar set on top of the Coeur à la Crème. When the waiter served the dessert, we would all peek through the small double door window to see if the lady-in-question said "yes". The recipe is simple to put together but does require a special Coeur à la Crème mold that is perforated to help the excess whey drain as it sits. If you do not care about the shape, you can skip the mold and suspend the mixture in the cheesecloth set inside a strainer or colander.

1. In a bowl, combine cream, vanilla, zest and seeds.

2. Using the immersion blended fitted with the whisk attachment, whisk until soft peaks form; refrigerate.

3. In a microwave-safe bowl, microwave the cream cheese for 30 seconds or until very soft; do not scorch it.

4. Using a spatula, stir the powdered sugar into the cream cheese until combined.

5. Fold the cream cheese mixture into the heavy cream mixture until combined.

6. Line a Coeur à la Crème mold (see tools page 9) with a cheesecloth so that the ends drape over the sides of the mold.

7. Place the mold on a plate.

8. Pour the mixture into the cheesecloth, fold the edges over the top and refrigerate overnight.

9. Discard the liquid, invert onto a plate and remove the cheesecloth.

10. Garnish with Raspberry Coulis and raspberries before serving.

Lemon Pudding Cakes

Makes 6 servings

Ingredients

¼ cup all purpose flour

¾ cup granulated sugar, divided

1 cup whole milk

3 large eggs, separated

Zest of 2 lemons

¼ cup fresh lemon juice

½ teaspoon vanilla extract

¼ cup unsalted butter, melted

¼ teaspoon kosher salt

1. Preheat oven to 325 degrees; apply non-stick spray to 6 individual ramekins.

2. In a large bowl, sift together the flour and 1/2 cup of sugar.

3. In a separate bowl, combine milk and egg yolks; mix using the immersion blender wand until combined.

4. Add zest, lemon juice, vanilla and butter to the milk mixture; whisk using the wand.

5. Add flour and sugar mixture to the milk mixture; whisk until combined then set aside.

6. In a completely clean and dry bowl, combine the egg whites and salt; whisk on high speed using the immersion blender fitted with the whisk attachment.

7. While continuing to whisk on high speed, add remaining sugar to the egg white mixture and whisk until soft peaks form.

8. Combine the egg white mixture with the milk mixture; fold using a spoon until combined (do not deflate the mixture).

9. Pour the batter into the prepared ramekins until almost full then place them in a roasting pan.

10. Add hot water to the roasting pan until halfway up the sides of the ramekins.

11. Bake for 30 minutes or until the top layer is set and golden brown.

12. Run a knife around the sides or each ramekin, invert onto a plate and serve warm.

Manjari Chocolate Tarts

Makes 6 tarts

Crust Ingredients

1¼ cups all purpose flour
¼ cup cocoa powder
¼ cup powdered sugar
½ cup unsalted butter, melted

Chocolate Filling

½ cup granulated sugar
1 teaspoon vanilla extract
5 large egg yolks
1½ cups bittersweet chocolate (such as Manjari), chopped
¾ cup unsalted butter
Maldon sea salt (optional)

1. Preheat oven to 350 degrees.

2. Apply non-stick spray to 6 individual tart pans; set aside.

3. Place all crust ingredients into a bowl; mix using your fingers.

4. Press and pat the dough evenly into the bottom and sides of the tart pans.

5. Place tart pans on a cookie sheet and bake for 15 minutes.

6. Let cool and set aside.

7. Reduce oven temperature to 300 degrees.

8. Place sugar, vanilla and egg yolks into a bowl.

9. Using the immersion blender wand, mix on low speed for 20 seconds; set aside.

10. In a microwave-safe bowl, combine chocolate and butter; microwave until melted and smooth.

11. Combine the chocolate mixture with the sugar mixture; mix using the wand until smooth.

12. Divide the mixture between the tart pans.

13. Bake for exactly 10 minutes, top with sea salt if desired and serve.

Morning Glory Muffins

Makes 12 muffins

Ingredients

1 cup carrot chunks
1 Granny Smith apple, quartered
½ cup pecans, toasted
2 large eggs
⅓ cup vegetable oil
1 teaspoon pure vanilla extract
1 cup all purpose flour
½ cup brown sugar
1 teaspoon baking soda

1 teaspoon ground cinnamon
¼ teaspoon ground ginger
¼ teaspoon nutmeg
¼ teaspoon allspice
½ teaspoon kosher salt
½ cup dark raisins
½ cup coconut flakes, toasted
½ cup cream cheese, softened
½ cup sweetened coconut flakes for topping

1. Preheat oven to 350 degrees.

2. Apply non-stick spray to a muffin tin and set aside.

3. Place carrots, apples and pecans into the immersion blender chopper bowl.

4. Pulse to chop into small pieces.

5. Transfer apple mixture to a bowl.

6. Add remaining ingredients, except cream cheese and coconut flakes for topping, to the bowl and stir using a spoon until uniform in color.

7. Divide the batter between the muffin tin wells until each is 3/4 full.

8. Bake for 20 minutes or until well risen and brown.

9. Remove and let cool.

10. Spread cream cheese on each muffin.

11. Top with coconut flakes and serve.

Mango Sorbet

Makes 4 servings

Ingredients

3 cups frozen mango
12 ounces mango nectar, divided

Being on the air at HSN is very exciting and very HOT. The stage lights are quite bright and emit heat which is why Wolf loves to eat this sorbet to cool off. He also likes it because it is naturally creamy and not too sweet. He loves it so much that I've seen him stash some sorbet on set to snack on after the show.

1. Place the mango and half of the nectar into the immersion blender chopper bowl.

2. Pulse until smooth.

3. Add more nectar to adjust the consistency if desired and pulse again.

4. Scoop sorbet into pretty serving dishes.

5. Serve immediately.

Marian's Tip:
Homemade sorbets like this are best enjoyed as soon as they are made. Commercial sorbets use stabilizers or special freezing techniques to keep them smooth over a long period of time. Since this recipe contains only two ingredients, the texture will turn icy if you store it in the freezer.

One Bowl Butter Cupcakes

Makes 18 cupcakes

Ingredients

1 cup unsalted butter, very soft
2⅓ cups granulated sugar
5 large eggs
3 cups cake flour
¾ teaspoon baking soda
2¼ teaspoons baking powder

2 teaspoons kosher salt
1 cup whole milk
1 cup sour cream
1 tablespoon vanilla extract
Swiss Meringue (see page 136)

1. Preheat oven to 350 degrees.

2. Line a cupcake tin with papers; set aside.

3. Place butter and sugar into the immersion blender chopper bowl; cream for 40 seconds.

4. Scrape the sides of the bowl, add the eggs and mix for an additional 20 seconds.

5. Remove the blade from the chopper bowl.

6. Add flour, baking soda, baking powder and salt to the chopper bowl; stir using a rubber spatula.

7. Add milk and sour cream to the chopper bowl; stir until incorporated.

8. Scrape the bowl, add the vanilla and stir again.

9. Divide the mixture between the cupcake tin wells until each is 3/4 full.

10. Bake for 20-25 minutes or until golden brown; let cool completely.

11. Frost with Swiss Meringue and serve.

Marian's Tip:
To make the Swiss Meringue pink like it is in the photo, add 3 drops of red food coloring while mixing the Swiss Meringue.

Orange Creamsicles

Makes 4 servings

Ingredients

4 scoops vanilla ice cream
Zest from 1 orange
1 cup fresh orange juice
1 teaspoon vanilla extract
¼ teaspoon Fiori Di Sicilia (see source page 140)
2 drops orange food coloring (optional)

Our house was always the neighborhood hangout and since I am the mother of boys, there were only boys at the house when they were young. The girls did not arrive until their late middle school years. One day, about a dozen boys were busy in the kitchen making milk shakes. They had almost every ingredient from my pantry out on the counter so that every boy could invent his "own" shake. I don't know which kid added a few drops of a wonderful extract I had in the pantry called Fiori Di Sicilia, but it is the perfect orange creamsicle flavor. Fiori Di Sicilia is Italian for 'flower of Sicily" and is a delightful distillation of citrus flowers and vanilla. We've been making shakes with it ever since. Freeze the mixture in little cups for true creamsicles.

1. Place all ingredients into the immersion blender chopper bowl.

2. Purée on high speed until a smooth consistency is achieved.

3. Divide mixture between small paper cups or popsicle molds.

4. Freeze for 1 hour.

5. Insert popsicle sticks into the center of each pop.

6. Freeze solid before serving.

Marian's Tip:
*For a less creamy version of this treat, substitute
4 scoops of orange sherbet for the vanilla ice cream.*

Plum Galette

Makes 2 servings

Dough Ingredients

1¼ cups all purpose flour
½ teaspoon kosher salt
½ cup unsalted butter, cold and cut into small cubes
2 tablespoons ice water

Toppings

6 large dark plums, thinly sliced
4 tablespoons granulated sugar
2 tablespoons unsalted butter

1. Place all dough ingredients into the immersion blender chopper bowl.

2. Pulse to combine; do not overmix (make sure you can still see bits of butter).

3. Squeeze some dough, if it keeps its shape, it is done. Add 1 teaspoon of water if the dough is too crumbly and dry.

4. Shape the dough into 2 flat disks, cover and chill for at least 1 hour or overnight.

5. Preheat oven to 400 degrees.

6. On a lightly floured surface, roll out the dough disks into 10-inch circles.

7. Transfer the circles to a parchment-lined cookie sheet.

8. Arrange the plum slices over each dough circle, leaving a 2-inch border.

9. Sprinkle with sugar and dot with butter.

10. Turn the border of each circle up over the plums and pat in place.

11. Bake for 25 minutes or until juices start to run and the pastry is brown.

12. Serve immediately.

Marian's Tip:
Try substituting the plums with peaches, apples, rhubarb or mango slices.

Homemade Sno Cones

Makes 4 servings

Raspberry Syrup

1½ cups frozen raspberries

⅓ cup water

⅔ cup granulated sugar

2 tablespoons lemon juice

4 cups ice cubes

Blueberry Syrup

1½ cups frozen blueberries

⅓ cup water

⅔ cup granulated sugar

2 tablespoons lemon juice

4 cups ice cubes

Lime Syrup

Zest of 2 limes

⅔ cup fresh lime juice

⅔ cup granulated sugar

2 drops green food coloring

4 cups ice cubes

Pineapple Syrup

1½ cups frozen pineapple chunks

⅓ cup water

⅔ cup granulated sugar

2 tablespoons lemon juice

4 cups ice cubes

1. Place desired syrup ingredients, except ice cubes into a medium saucepan.

2. Bring to a boil over medium-high heat.

3. Remove from heat.

4. Strain through a fine mesh strainer into a storage container and keep cool.

5. Place ice cubes into the immersion blender chopper bowl.

6. Pulse on high to crush the ice.

7. Scoop ice into sno cone cups.

8. Top each sno cone with 2 tablespoons of syrup and serve.

White Chocolate Grasshopper Pie

Makes 8 servings

Crust Ingredients

6 tablespoons unsalted and melted butter, divided
30 chocolate wafers

Filling

2½ ounces white chocolate chips
1 cup heavy cream
1 packet (2½ teaspoons) unflavored gelatin
¼ cup whole milk
2 large egg yolks

2 large whole eggs
2 tablespoons granulated sugar
¼ cup crème de menthe liqueur
½ teaspoon peppermint extract

1. Preheat oven to 350 degrees; coat a 9-inch pie pan with 2 tablespoons of butter.

2. Place the wafers into the immersion blender chopper bowl; chop into fine crumbs then add remaining butter and pulse to combine.

3. Transfer crumbs to the pie pan, pat into the bottom and sides of the pan and bake for 10 minutes or until set and dry; let cool and set aside.

4. In a microwave-safe bowl, combine the chocolate chips and cream.

5. Microwave for 3 minutes or until hot; stir to melt the chocolate then let rest until cool.

6. In a small bowl, combine gelatin and milk; stir and set aside.

7. In a separate bowl, combine egg yolks, eggs and sugar; place it over medium heat in a double boiler containing 2 inches of simmering water.

8. Hand whisk until very hot without scrambling the eggs then remove from heat.

9. Using the immersion blender fitted with the whisk attachment, whisk on high speed for 2 minutes or until mixture is thick.

10. Set the bowl of gelatin over the boiling water until dissolved.

11. Whisk gelatin and remaining ingredients into the egg mixture; let cool.

12. Whip the chocolate mixture until soft peaks form then fold it into the egg mixture without deflating it.

13. Pour mixture into the pie crust and refrigerate for 2 hour or until set.

14. Cut into 8 slices and serve.

ETCETERA

Sweet Potato Purée with Gingersnap Cookies

Makes 4 servings

Ingredients

2 pounds sweet potatoes, peeled and cut into 1-inch chunks
4 tablespoons unsalted butter
6 gingersnap cookies
2 tablespoons granulated sugar
2 teaspoons fresh lemon juice
½ cup heavy cream or whole milk
Kosher salt to taste
Freshly cracked black pepper to taste

Wolf serves this dish with a beautiful pork loin that is stuffed with dried apricots, prunes and cranberries. The purée is silky smooth and wonderfully flavored from the gingersnap cookies. Since sweet potatoes do not contain the same type of starch as regular potatoes, they do not turn "gluey" when puréed. You can purée them for a long time until ultra-smooth. Serve with some extra crumbled gingersnap cookies for a texture contrast.

1. Steam the sweet potatoes in a steamer basket for 20 minutes or until very tender.

2. Transfer potatoes to the immersion blender chopper bowl.

3. Add butter, cookies, sugar and lemon juice to the chopper bowl.

4. Purée on high speed for 30 seconds.

5. Scrape the bowl, add the cream and purée until smooth.

6. Taste and adjust the seasoning with salt and pepper as desired.

7. Serve immediately.

Marian's Tip:
If you do not have gingersnap cookies, just add a tablespoon of light brown sugar, 2 teaspoons of molasses, a half teaspoon of dry ginger and a half teaspoon of cinnamon.

Cauliflower Mashers

Makes 4 servings

Ingredients

1 large head of cauliflower, cut into florets
1 cup chicken stock
½ cup whole milk or half & half
½ teaspoon lemon juice

3 tablespoons unsalted butter
Kosher salt to taste
Freshly cracked pepper to taste

These mashers are popular with those who are watching their carbohydrate consumption. They are a surprisingly good stand-in for regular mashed potatoes. Cauliflower is a much overlooked vegetable that is versatile as well as adaptable and deserves much more respect. Unlike potatoes, cauliflower does not contain starch and is perfect for puréeing with the immersion blender. You can blend it for a long time and get it silky smooth without turning "gluey" the way potatoes do. The small amount of lemon juice helps to keep the cauliflower nice and white.

1. In a large saucepan, combine all ingredients, except butter, salt and pepper; bring to a boil over medium heat.

2. Reduce heat to a simmer, cover with a lid and cook for 15 minutes or until fork tender.

3. Drain most of the liquid, reserve it and set aside.

4. Using the immersion blender wand on low speed, start puréeing the cauliflower then increase the speed to high and purée until very smooth.

5. Blend in the butter and enough reserved liquid until a soft texture is achieved (the mixture should mound slightly but spread out a bit when spooned onto a plate).

6. Taste and adjust the seasoning with salt and pepper as desired.

7. Serve immediately.

Marian's Tip:
Form any leftovers into patties, roll them in panko then sauté them in a little butter until brown on the outside and soft on the inside. They are perfect served alongside roast beef or pork chops.

Cranberry Relish

Makes 2 cups

Ingredients

2 cups fresh cranberries
1 small orange, cut into 8 wedges with the peel on
⅔ cup granulated sugar or to taste

Thanksgiving is my favorite holiday because it is a day solely dedicated to food. Turkey is my favorite meat and the glorious smells coming from the kitchen makes for an even greater holiday. I serve this relish alongside the canned cranberry jelly because I love them both. This relish packs a huge, refreshing flavor and the smell is terrific as well. The immersion blender chopper bowl is a real time saver when it comes to chopping, which is nice on a busy day such as Thanksgiving. Make some extra relish and give it away as a gift in a pretty jar.

1. Place all ingredients into the immersion blender chopper bowl.

2. Pulse on high until well blended.

3. Scrape the sides of the chopper bowl and continue to pulse until no large pieces remain.

4. Transfer chopper bowl contents to a jar or a container with a lid.

5. Refrigerate for at least 2 hours before serving.

6. Stir before serving.

7. Store relish covered and refrigerated for up to 2 weeks.

Marian's Tip:
For a twist, add some toasted walnuts to this recipe.

Cranberry Relish

Homemade Peanut Butter

Makes ½ cup

Ingredients
1 cup roasted peanuts
1 tablespoon water

I am a peanut butter junkie and this recipe is easy to make thanks to the immersion blender. When I was little, making peanut butter was an all day process. Shelling the peanuts was alot of work but I really liked doing it. I never got tired of sitting on the porch next to my mom and siblings, chatting and shelling those tiny African peanuts. After the shelling, we toasted the peanuts, leaving the red skins on. Finally, we ran them through an old hand-cranked meat grinder that we clamped onto a table on the back porch. We took turns grinding because the big, stubborn handle would tire us quickly. It took 7 times through the grinder to make smooth peanut butter. The repeated grinding and heat from the friction would gradually melt the peanuts into a smooth consistency. We never added salt or sugar to our peanut butter but you certainly can if you want yours to taste similar to the store bought variety.

1. Place the peanuts into the immersion blender chopper bowl.

2. Chop for 15 seconds.

3. Shake the chopper bowl then chop for an additional 15 seconds.

4. Add water to the chopper bowl and purée until fairly smooth.

5. Adjust the consistency by adding water if desired.

6. Transfer the peanut butter to a covered jar or container.

7. Store peanut butter covered and refrigerated for up to 3 days.

Marian's Tips:
You can use the same technique to make other nut butters. Toasted pecans, cashews, hazelnuts, macadamia nuts or almonds all work well.
Also, try adding some chocolate chips to make some delicious chocolate flavored nut butter.

Homemade Mayonnaise

Makes 2 cups

Ingredients

2 large eggs
2 cups vegetable oil
2 teaspoons kosher salt
1 tablespoon dry mustard powder
1 tablespoon white vinegar
Pinch of white pepper (optional)

When I was little, my mom had the coolest contraption for making mayonnaise. It was a glass jug with measuring lines on the side. It had a flat metal lid with a hand cranked egg beater on top and a funnel for adding oil. The hardest part was turning the handle long and fast enough to blend the oil into the mayonnaise. It was worth all the effort even though our arms ached afterwards. Make sure you use the freshest eggs you can find when making this recipe. In Africa, we raised our own chickens of the Rhode Island Red variety. We even named them and treated them like pets so we knew that their eggs were as fresh as possible.

1. Place all ingredients into the immersion blender beaker.

2. Position the immersion blender wand at the bottom of the beaker.

3. Turn the immersion blender on high speed while keeping the wand at the bottom for 5 seconds.

4. Move the wand up and down to emulsify.

5. Store mayonnaise covered and refrigerated for up to 1 week.

Marian's Tips:
The white pepper is a classical French ingredient in mayonnaise but I leave it optional because I personally don't like it. Also, try adding some garlic cloves, pesto, sun-dried tomatoes or fresh herbs to make a delicious variation.

Raspberry Coulis

Makes 1½ cups

Ingredients

1 bag (12 ounces) frozen raspberries, thawed
⅔ cup granulated sugar

Coulis is the general French term for a thick, puréed sauce that is not cooked. Originally, it referred to a thick shellfish sauce but now refers to sauces made with fruits or even tomatoes. Regardless of the name, this sauce is a fresh burst of flavor and an indispensable recipe that I use everywhere. It is the sauce that we top the rice pudding with for the HSN shows. It is incredibly easy to make, very versatile and freezes well. Sometimes I strain out the seeds using a Chinois (a very fine French cone-shaped strainer) and other times I just leave them in because they look pretty. For an emergency dessert, layer this sauce with sweetened whipped cream into pretty goblets for a stunning layered raspberry mousse.

1. Place the ingredients into a bowl.

2. Using the immersion blender wand, purée until very smooth.

3. Scrape the sides of the bowl and continue to blend for an additional 30 seconds or until all of the sugar has dissolved.

4. Strain through a fine mesh strainer to remove seeds if desired.

5. Store sauce covered and refrigerated for up to 5 days or freeze for up to 3 months.

Marian's Tip:
Use different fruits to make different flavored coulis. Kiwi and almost all berries will work using the same fruit to sugar ratio. For peaches, try adding half of the sugar as peaches are not as tart as berries. Always taste and adjust the sugar to your liking.

Chocolate Ganache

Makes 3½ cups

Ingredients

2 cups heavy cream
2½ cups good quality bittersweet chocolate chips (see source page 140)
1 teaspoon vanilla extract
¼ cup black coffee

Everyone should know about ganache. It is that magical chocolaty filling, frosting and glaze all mixed into one amazing recipe. The incredible texture is a result of the cream softening the chocolate and the chocolate stiffening the cream. The immersion blender makes it easy to achieve an ultra-silky texture. The quality of the chocolate makes a big difference in this recipe so use the best you can find (see source page 140).

Marian's Tip:
To make milk chocolate ganache, substitute milk chocolate for the bittersweet chocolate, reduce the cream to 1 cup and omit the coffee.

1. In a 4-quart saucepan over medium heat, cook the cream for 6 minutes or until steamy hot.

2. Remove from heat and add remaining ingredients.

3. Let rest for 5 minutes to soften the chocolate.

4. Using the immersion blender wand, mix on low speed until well blended and the mixture turns shiny.

5. Scrape the saucepan and blend for an additional 10 seconds.

6. The ganache is now ready for use as a topping or glaze. You can also chill it and use it as a fudgy frosting or filling (you can microwave it back into a glaze consistency if you desire).

7. Store ganache covered and refrigerated for up to 5 days.

Veggie Baby Food

Makes 2 - 4 servings

Potato Baby Food

2 medium potatoes, peeled

⅔ cup water

(cut potatoes into 1-inch chunks then steam until fork tender)

Beet Baby Food

3 medium fresh beets

¼ cup water

(cut beets into 1-inch chunks then steam until fork tender)

Carrot Baby Food

3 medium carrots, trimmed and peeled

½ cup water

(cut carrots into 1-inch sections then steam until fork tender)

Pea Baby Food

1 cup frozen peas, thawed

⅓ cup water

(the peas do not need to be steamed)

Making your own baby food is easy and so much better for your little one. It is also much less expensive. I suggest buying quality organic produce from your farmer's market. Using the immersion blender to purée the vegetables is a snap and you can easily adjust the texture to suit your growing baby. In the beginning, make the purée as smooth as possible, even straining the food after puréeing. Change the texture gradually as your baby starts growing and when your baby gets a couple of teeth, start leaving it a bit chunkier.

1. Place desired vegetable and water into the immersion beaker.

2. Using the immersion blender wand, purée until smooth.

3. If you desire a smoother consistency, push the mixture through a fine mesh strainer.

4. Serve immediately or freeze in individual portions for later use.

Marian's Tip:
I found that the easiest way to steam vegetables is in the steamer basket of my Wolfgang Puck rice cooker. Just add 2 inches of water to the rice cooker insert, fit the rice cooker with the steamer basket and add the vegetables to the basket. Check for doneness after about 5 minutes and continue steaming if needed.

Fruit Baby Food

Makes 2 - 4 servings

Peach Baby Food

1 cup frozen peaches, thawed
¼ cup water

Blueberry Baby Food

1 cup frozen blueberries, thawed
¼ cup water

Apple Baby Food

1 Golden Delicious apple, peeled and cored
¼ cup water
(cut apples into quarters then steam until fork tender)

Guava Baby Food

4 guavas, quartered
¼ cup water
(steam guava until fork tender)

I never bought jarred baby food for my boys when they were babies. Almost all of their food was either mashed using a fork or put through a plastic food mill contraption where you press a small handle to push the food through a perforated lid. While the mill worked well, it was hard to turn. I usually gave up after a few turns and gratefully handed it over to my big, burly husband to finish. If we had owned an immersion blender, life would have been so much easier. I suggest making your baby food at home using the best quality ingredients so you know exactly what's in it.

1. Place desired fruit and water into the immersion beaker.

2. Using the immersion blender wand, purée until smooth.

3. If you desire a smoother consistency, push the mixture through a fine mesh strainer.

4. Serve immediately or freeze in individual portions for later use.

Marian's Tip:
The easiest way to freeze individual portions of baby food is to use silicone ice cube trays. Just fill them to the top with baby food, cover and freeze. Once frozen, pop them out into a plastic zipper bag and store the food in the freezer. The silicone makes for much easier removal since you can just turn it inside out.

Gluten Free Mall
4927 Sonoma Hwy, Ste C1,
Santa Rosa, CA 65409
(866) 575-3720
www.glutenfreemall.com

all ingredients for gluten-free baking

Fortune Products Inc.
205 Hickory Creek Rd.
Marble Falls, TX 78654
(830) 693-61111
www.accusharp.com

hand-held Accusharp knife sharpeners

D&G Occansions
625 Herndon Ave
Orlando, FL 32803
(407) 894-4458
www.dandgoccasions.com

Butter-vanilla extract by Magic Line,
pure vanilla extract, citric acid, pure
fruit oils, professional food coloring,
ultra thin flexible spatulas, unusual
birthday candles, candy making and
baking supplies

Chocosphere
P.O. Box 2237
Tualatin, OR 97062
(877) 992-4626
www.chocosphere.com

excellent quality cocoa (Callebaut),
chocolates, jimmies and sprinkles

Rolling Pin Kitchen Emporium
P.O. Box 21798
Long Beach, CA 90801
customerservice@rollingpin.com
www.rollingpin.com

baker's ammonia, cheesecloths, inexpensive
"harp" shaped vegetable peelers and other
kitchen tools

Whole Foods
550 Bowie St.
Austin, TX 78703
(512) 499-4455
www.wholefoods.com

grains, citric acid,
natural and organic
products, xanthan gum,
gluten-free baking items

S

Sage & Red Onion Focaccia 78
Sage & Walnut Pesto 20
Salt Cod Fritters 50
Sam's Pancakes 76
Slime 138
Southern Deviled Eggs 52
Strawberry Kiwi Kooler 62
Strawberry Rhubarb Bavarian Cream 92
Sweet Potato Purée & Gingersnap Cookies 119
Swiss Meringue 136

Salad

Chicken Salad 54

Salsa

Corn Salsa 28
Estela's Tomato Salsa 32
Green Apple & Curry Salsa 34
Mango Salsa 26
Peach Salsa 30

Smoothie

Citrus Slushy 64
Strawberry Kiwi Kooler 62

Sorbet

Chocolate Sorbet 96
Mango Sorbet 106

Soup

Borscht 46
Butternut Squash Soup 37
Creamy Zucchini Soup 48
Pea Soup 42
Potage Parmentier 44
Roasted Tomato Basil Soup 40
Zellwood Sweet Corn Soup 38

Strawberry

Old Fashioned Strawberry Milk Shake 60
Strawberry Kiwi Kooler 62
Strawberry Rhubarb Bavarian Cream 92

T

Tart

Manjari Chocolate Tarts 102
Plum Galette 112

V

Veggie Baby Food 132

Vinaigrette

Brown Butter Vinaigrette 24
Prickly Pear Vinaigrette 22

W

White Chocolate Grasshopper Pie 116
Whole Wheat Flatbread Crackers 80
Whole Wheat Pizza Dough 82

Y

Yorkshire Pudding

Individual Yorkshire Pudding 74

Z

Zellwood Sweet Corn Soup 38

Zucchini

Creamy Zucchini Soup 48

For more of Marian's tips and ideas, please visit:

www.mariangetz.com